Top Tricks

Karl Rohnke

KENDALL/HUNT PUBLISHING COMPANY
4050 Westmark Drive   Dubuque, Iowa 52002

MW01533616

TOP TRICKS©

Karl Rohnke

Participants in adventure workshops consistently ask, "Are all these activities written down somewhere?" My answer has been consistently, "Yes, but I'm not sure where." Even after compiling the information below, I still don't know off the top of my head where, but at least now we can look it up. The following list of *Top Tricks* are those adventure curriculum activities that I use on a regular basis; i.e., my favorites.

Key to Source Books

BBA	— Bottomless Bag Again!?
BB	— Bottomless Baggie
SB	— Silver Bullets
CT&C	— Cowstails & Cobras II
BOTs	— Bag of Tricks
QS	— QuickSilver
FS1	— Fun Stuff #1

Key to Activity Use

Outdoor Activity	— O
Indoor Activity	— I
Indoor/Outdoor	— I/O
Activity Level High	— S (sweat)
Activity Level Med.	— MS
Activity Level Low	— NS
Needs Props	— P
Needs Min. Props	— MP
No Props Necessary	— NP

All the above books can be ordered from Kendall/Hunt Publishing Company. Call the following number to order; or for more information:

1-800-228-0810

Activity Key Interpretation

Indoor Activity and **Outdoor Activity** are relative terms, because most of the time a game or initiative problem can be pursued either indoors or outdoors.

No Sweat means that your heart rate will probably not increase as the result of participation in the designated activity. **Medium Sweat** indicates that at some point during the game or activity your heart rate will increase, and on hot days a bead of sweat or two might might appear upon your brow. **Sweat** means that at full participation you will be breathing hard, your heart rate will be high and you will experience copious perspiration.

No Props Necessary means just that. **Needs Minimum Props** indicates that you will be using easily transportable items during the game or initiative. When you see **Needs Props** be set to transport (or not transport!) some heavy or awkward items around.

A brief description of terms you need to know concerning adventure programming:

Adventure Games—Often called New Games. (Any *old* game that has been rediscovered or creatively embellished is a *new* game.) These games are selectively used to encourage cooperation, communication, and a trusting approach toward one another.

Initiative Problems—A fabricated bit of fantasy presented in a solve-the-problem format. It is the facilitators function to present the problem in an entertaining manner, setting parameters for operation and safety, then stepping back to let the group work on and hopefully solve the problem. Recognize that the process is more significant than the result.

Trust Activities—Presented situations that lead toward the building of physical and emotional trust among members of the group, recognizing that building trust takes time and effort while destroying trust can be accomplished in seconds.

Challenge By Choice—Presenting a challenging problem or situation, then letting the student decide *when*, not *if*, they will make an attempt. Contrary to some people's interpretation, CBC is not an invitation to cop out, rather an opportunity to take a breather, watch others make an attempt, then go for it themselves to the extent that is satisfying to the individual.

F.U.N.N.—To be succinct, FUNN is an acronym for Functional Understanding's Not Necessary. There doesn't have to be a reason for fun, it is an end in itself, a benefit of being alive.

Failing Forward—The words *fail* and *failing* are not well received in our society. So much so that people often refuse to try something new for fear of failing. Success is predominently made up of failures, lots of them. Successful people are those individuals not afraid to fail. So, *failing forward* indicates that you (or someone) did not reach their goal, but in trying you (they) learned something, and you're "failing" in the right direction toward eventual success.

THE ACTIVITIES ───────────

Here's how to use the following list. **STOP** ! Don't you dare just go visually thrashing and perusing about. I spent much more time than I wanted to organizing this stuff (my one-minded compulsive side), so pay attention.

Key into the keys and icons. Each activity/game has a:

- Key to the source—what book and what page
- Key to activity use—what venue and how strenuous
- Key to programmatic use—ice breaker, game, initiative problem, etc.

Acronyms—I, NS, MP
BB-16; FS1
Good activity to teach brainstorming techniques. Pick and choose your acronyms carefully so that they "fit" the age and maturity levels of your group.

Add On Tag—O, S, NP
*BA-81; SB-42 See **Tusker** (MP needed)*
A large grass field is an ideal venue for this running game. The use of "tusks" (ethafoam bats) as tagging devices is well received by most players.

Ah-So-Ko—I/O, NS, NP
FS1
When you present this game be animated and zany. This is a FUNN game.

Alienation—I/O, NS, MP
QS-98
If the game *Killer* is not well received because of the title, try *Alienation*, it's practically the same game with a different caption.

All Catch—I/O, NS, MP
BBA-80; BB-2
This is a useful introductory game that requires minimum skill, and offers a team challenge. Can also be played with Twirlies. *Up Chuck* and *All Catch* are practically the same game.

4

Almost Infinite Circle—I/O, NS, MP
SB-131
Use as a introductory ploy. The activity demands closeness, but not too close. The solution is a real puzzler.

Amazon—O, MS, P
SB-137
An initiative problem for a group that can handle a demanding challenge. This one will not fit in your game bag.

Ankle Biters—I/O, S, MP
BBA-78
This is one of my all time favorite games; flat out fun at a variety of levels.

Asteroids—I/O, S, MP
BBA-77
Use as a lead up to *Ankle Biters*. Played by itself it's just a glorified and innocuous version of *Bombardment*.

Auto Tag—I/O, S, MP
QS-100
Another tag game with a twist. It's worth a try.

Back Stabbers—I/O, S, MP
QS-101
This is kind of an anti-trust game. Good fun, but be careful of when and where you use it.

Balance Broom—I/O, MS, MP
SB-164; CT&C-44
There is an other-worldly (Todo El Dizzy) sensation to be had here. Announce that dizziness can trigger an epileptic seizure. Be a good spotter.

Balloon Frantic—I, S, MP
BBA-66; SB-19
If the principal is observing your adventure class today, use this activity. Very active and visual.

Balloon Trolleys—I, MS, MP
QS-49
Considerably harder than it reads. Go for the challenge and finish up with *Fire in the Hole*.

Balls Galore—I/O, NS, P
SB-175
Good summer camp activity or for a teen night.

"Bang . . . "—I/O, NS, NP
BBA-45
Another of the, "Where's the key" genre of games.

Bean Bag Tag—I/O, S, MP
QS-103
You gotta have a mess of bean bags. This is not an easy tag game.

Bends, The—I/O, MS, NP
QS-240
A variation of *Squat Thrust*. Play compassionately. Good for building trust.

Blind Fold Line Up—I/O, NS, NP
BBA-98
Make sure this activity is in your conceptual bag of tricks. This is the best no prop initiative I know of for building trust and communication, plus it's a plethora of fun. Video this activity so the group can enjoy the action.

Blindfold Soccer—I/O, S, MP
SB-69
Definitely a trust builder. Discourage high kicks. Use blindfolds.

Blind Polygon—I/O, NS, MP
CT&C-81
Good for all ages to build trust and a useful sense of commu-nication. Blindfolds may be necessary for younger groups. Observe the group carefully for later debriefing scenarios.

Body Sac—I/O, MS, MP
BB-28, BBA-27
Introduce and demonstrate this game. People like the chal-lenge but you have to get them interested and started. Perfect for the people (like me) who can't kick a hackey sack twice in succession.

Boffer Bonkers—I, S, MP
BBA-73
This is the most aerobic (becoming anaerobic) one-on-one activity that I know. Give it a try yourself and suck some serious wind.

Booop—I, MS, MP
SB-49; BBA-67
I can't think of a better game for young elementary students to identify body parts (basic anatomy) while working together. Useful for any age; kiddies through corporate.

Bottom Line—I/O, MS, P
BB-15
Requires some setting up, but the team action becomes infectious.

Bottoms Up—I/O, MS, NP
CT&C-39; BBA-6; SB-159
So how's the triceps feel after this one? Good one-on-one laugher. Use as part of your "on the floor" series of quick hitters.

Bridge It—I, NS, P
SB-127; BBA-112
This is a sophisticated initiative problem; perfect for the corporate crowd.

Buddy Ropes—I/O, NS, MP
BB-46; QS-220
Inexpensive props, particularly useful to increase the number of participants in the initiative *Knots* or *Tangle*. See also *Human Overhand*.

Bugs in my Cup . . .—I, NS, MP
FS1
Another, "Where's the key" problem.

Bump—I/O, MS, P
SB-68
Unselfconscious touch, team work, party game, laughter . . .

Bumpity-Bump-Bump—I/O, MS, NP
BBA-9; QS-84
A name reminder game that moves quickly.

Catch 10—0, S, MP
SB-64
A "skilled" game. The format can be frustrating for folks who don't throw or catch well. Tons of action.

Categories—I/O, NS, NP
BBA-143, QS-85
Tuck this one into your adventure bag of tricks. Use with any size group to break some ice and learn more about your playmates. Useful for choosing up sides.

Caught Ya Peekin'—I/O, NS, NP
BBA-125
A lightweight, quickie. You have to be in the mood for some nonsense. Rules? What rules?

Chronological Line Up—I/O, NS, NP
SB-163
A subtle trust exercise. Check the teeth, works every time.

Circle The Circle—I/O, MS, P
BBA-115; SB-60
People like this activity, probably because they can't hula the hoop!

Circle Slap—I, MS, NP
FS1
A variation of *Knee Slap,* down and dirty, prone on the floor.

Claydoughnary—I, NS, MP
QS-109
A hands-on version of Pictionary. Get yourself some of that great smelling Play Dough.

Co-op Competition—I/O, MS, NP
BBA-5; SB-94
Cooperative competition? Here it is. Make it work.

Comet Ball Boccie—O, MS, P
QS-241
Just like it says, Boccie using Comet Balls. I like this game, and I'm good at it.

Comet Balls—O, MS, P
BBA-68; SB-25; BB-90; QS-242
If you haven't thrown a Comet Ball, go do it right now. Everyone loves *Comet Balls.* Don't confuse these with commercial Fox Tails, it's like comparing a Porsche to a VW with the Comet Balls getting the nod.

Coming and Going of the Rain— I/O, MS, NP
SB-92

This is a classic outdoor education group activity. Try the hands-on technique.

Commons—I, MS, NP
QS-110

I've rarely seen this "work", but it's a heck of a lot of fun trying. This is an effective activity to use at the close of a program.

Compass Walk—O, MS, MP
SB-176

One of the best open field activities I know of to emphasize trust. Remember to try the *Hansel and Gretel* variation.

Commandant—O, S, P
SB-73; BBA-81

A specialized night-time activity. In the right area on a warm night it's a winner.

Count Off: 1-20—I/O, NS, NP
B-179; BBA-95

Gotta have this one in your back pocket. It's an effective quickie initiative that you can present anywhere.

Cranial Snatch It—I/O, MS, MP
BB-69

You can only play this crazy game with *Comet Balls.* Get a photo of the action, because nobody will believe you otherwise.

Dangle Duo Double Use—I/O, MS, P
QS-197

This is *Bottom Line* and *Moon Ball* combined with the use of a Dangle Do. This is a team effort activity.

Debriefing—Concept
BBA-279; CT&C-21-27

Debriefing (processing, reviewing) isn't an activity, but you better know what it's all about otherwise all these activities are just that, recreational activities. Do some reading about this.

Diminishing Load—I/O, S, NP
SB-138
The answer to this initiative problem is not complex, but it's going to make your heart pump a bit harder. Watch out for back injuries.

Disc Jockeys—I/O, MS, P
BBA-226
This is a ropes course or gymnasium initiative problem; and a good swinging time. People love problems that involve a swing rope.

Dog Shake—I/O, MS, NP
SB-168; CT&C-36; BBA-15
If you can present this warm-up by demonstrating the action you expect from the participants, you have achieved the level of ZANY that I speak of so often.

Do-I-Go—I/O, MS, P
BBA-227; QS -54
Another ropes course initiative that requires a swing rope or two.

Dollar Drop—I/O, NS, MP
QS-238
If you have five minutes before the end of class, try this, "I'll bet you can't" problem. Got a dollar?

Dollar Jump—I/O, NS, MP
SB-174; BBA-31
Same as above, but the task is a bit more physical. Spot for the kamikaze participants.

Don't Touch Me!—I/O, MS, MP
QS-56
An effective initiative problem that highlights leadership issues and the virtue of listening more than talking.

Elbow Tag—I/O, S, NP
BBA-2
A thinking person's tag game, but you still have to run.

Everybody Up—I/O, MS, NP
CT&C-39; BBA-96, SB-100
An initiative problem that starts with two people working together trying to accomplish a task and ends up with everyone in the group trying to do the same thing.

Everybody's IT—IT/0, S, NP
BBA-1
Everyone's favorite tag game; doesn't last long either.

F Words—I, NS, MP
BBA-124
Requires some prep time, but then moves rapidly.

Five-A-Side Flatball—I/0, MS, MP
CT&C-64; BBA-89
I invented this one in Australia after all my beach balls started to leak. A fast moving, atypical, blatantly competitive game

Fast Draw—0, MS, MP
SB-28 ; BBA-30
This is just plain fun in the sun, with a smidgen of goal orientation.

FFEACH—I/0, MS, NP
QS-114
A Steve Butler original. If you like charades you will like this more.

Fire-in-the-Hole—I, MS, MP
SB-51; BBA-67; QS-199
A game for all seasons and no reasons. Enjoy popping balloons? Here's your game.

Flip Me the Bird Tag—I/0, S, P
SB-155; BBA-3
Saying the name of the game is as much fun as playing. Using rubber chickens is better than tossing knotted towels.

Four Way Tug-O-War
See Unholy Alliance

Frantic—I, S, P
SB-18; BBA-65
This tennis ball game was the precursor to *Balloon Frantic*. Mucho activity with beau coups balls.

Frog Wars—I, S, P
BBA-84
Fantasy and fun in a full gym format. Lots of activity, consequence, and laughter.

Funnelator—O, MS, P
BBA-146
You can buy a commercial balloon launcher, but it's more fun and satisfying to make your own. Here's how.

Great Egg Drop—I/O, NS, P
BBA-111
Another initiative that applies well to the corporate crowd and just about anyone else. Everyone likes to see (anticipate) eggs breaking.

Gooney Likes . . .—I, NS, NP
BBA-125
What Gooney likes is an example of vertical vs. lateral thinking. Simple but confounding.

Gooney Variations—I, NS, NP
QS-251
If you like Gooney you will like the variations.

Group Juggling—I/O, MS, MP
SB-112; CT&C-84; QS-201
Use Group Juggling as an introduction to *Warp Speed;* nice combination. One of the best actually.

Hammeroids—I, NS, P
QS-162
I'd try this one just because of the name. A center of gravity forehead slapper. How does it do that?

Hands Down—I, NS, NP
BBA-46; SB-53
Practice your presentation a couple times before demonstrating to a group. This puzzler is an excellent example of vertical/lateral thinking.

Hansel & Gretel—O, NS, P
QS-200
To be used only with an activity called the *Compass Walk.*

Have You Ever . . . ?—I, NS/MS, P/NP
BBA-127; BB-93; QS-224
The reason I'm wishy-washy about the keys above is that this activity can be approached in different ways; check it out. This is one of my all-time favorite games.

Heads & Tails Tag—I/O, S, MP
*BBA-6; QS-91; See **Transformer Tag***
A unique start to the game and then it's run-run-run as usual.

Help Me, Rhonda—I, NS, P
BBA-45
The Beach Boys affiliation has nothing to do with the game, it's just fun to say. The game is a paper and pencil quick thinking bash of chosen categories. Is that enough to turn you off?

Hog Call—I/O, MS, NP
SB-98; QS-202
Use this game as a very loud means of getting to know one another.

Hooper—O, S, MP
BBA-79
Hooper's OK, but *UDT (Ultimate Deck Tennis)* is better.

Hop Box—
*See **Jumping Jack Flash***
Well . . . go see it.

Hopping—I/O, S, NP
CT&C-30-33
A unique warm up sequence. Be prepared to breathe—hard.

Hospital Tag—I/O, S, NP
*BBA-2; See **Sore Spot Tag***
Kind of like *Everybody's IT*, but this tag game lasts longer.

How're Ya Doin . . . ?—I/O, NS, NP
BBA-51
A low key introduction to zaniness. The success of this game depends upon your enthusiastic presentation.

How We Differ—I, NS, P
QS-77

Human Camera—O, NS, NP
BBA-18
A classic outdoor education activity and a dandy introduction to trusting.

Human Ladder—I/O, MS, P
BBA-14; SB-113
Definitely a trust activity. Proctor this one well to make sure that it remains a trust activity.

Human Overhand—I/O, NS, P
FS1
This is a very deceptive initiative problem. Don't be sucked in by its apparent simplicity.

Hustle Handle (Hustle Bustle)— I/O, NS, NP
BB-96; CT&C-66; QS-87
I like to use *Hustle Handle* as an introductory activity, and as an example of how ludicrous competition can become.

"I Trust You, but . . . "—I/O, MS, NP
*BBA-15; SB-91; See **Yeah, but . . .***
Intense trust activity. Try jogging the length of a football field. Keep on top of this activity; don't let the participants fool around.

Impulse Genre—I/O, NS, NP
BBA-141; CT&C-69
All of the impulse variations provide good warm up or introductory material. Included are *Hustle Handle, Hand Squeeze, Clapping, Whistling.*

Inch Worm—I/O, MS, NP
SB-158; CT&C-38; BBA-150
More warm up stuff. Provides an opportunity for unselfconscious touch and some low key competition.

Invisible Jump Rope—I/O, S, NP
SB-157; BBA-7
Creative warm up activity. Be animated and histrionic while demonstrating the jumping action. No ropes? Right!

Is This It?—I, NS, P
BB-52
A mind puzzler. Requires lateral thinking. Practice presenting this one before you try a live audience.

It Ain't Me Babe—I, NS, NP
QS-80
One-on-one introductions without speaking. A miming extravaganza.

Italian Golf—0, MS, MP
BBA-86; CT&C-67

I'm not sure why people like this game so much; perhaps the unique catching position. Good game for teaching golfing etiquette and associated vocabulary. "Fore" "Dog-leg left" "Green to Tee," etc.

I've Got the Beat—I, NS, NP
BBA-47

Another, "Where's the key" game.

Jumping Jack Flash—I/O, S, P
QS-167 See **Hop Box**

There aren't many games that work well with over 100 people; this one does. Functions well with smaller groups too.

Junk Yard—0, NS, P
BB-49 ; QS-168

Good initiative activity, but you have to be in the right place and have lots of "junk" to work with. Refer to *Stepping Stones* for a similar initiative situation that requires less props.

Kangaroo Catch—0, S, MP
QS-121

Kangaroos. Hopping. Right! Add A few hula hoops and a soupcon of rules for a unique move-from-A-to-B game.

Key Punch—I/O, S, P
QS-169

Currently a very popular corporate initiative from Australia. Demands decision making, speed, agility, leadership . . . all the good stuff.

Killer—I/O, MS, NP
SB-52

Call it whatever you want to but the game is still *Killer*. Very popular with workshop participants, particularly the 24 hour version.

King/Queen Me—I/O, MS, NP
QS-245

Like *Traffic Jam* and *2X4*, but different, harder maybe.

Knee Slap—I/O, NS, NP
BB-1; QS-246

See *Circle Slap*. A useful exercise for promoting unselfconscious touch and initiating spontaneous laughter.

Knots—See Tangle

Maze—O, NS, P
QS-203 & 232
A blindfolded low ropes course activity. Put up/take down capability and easy to fabricate amongst the right trees (lots of them).

Medley Relay—I/O, MS, MP
FS1
A group relay involving a series of individually performed forward momentum actions: hopping, jumping, cart wheels, diving . . .

Mine Field—I/O, NS, P
BBA-52; QS-148 & 205
Workshop participants regularly rate this initiative as one of their favorites. An eyes closed, partner oriented activity.

Monarch—I/O, S, MP
BB-13; QS-125
Lots of running and inadvertent teamwork.

Monster—I/O, S, NP
SB-132
A useful initiative problem for smaller distinct groups. Be alert for human overloading and potential back injuries.

Moonball—I/O, MS, MP
SB-31; BBA-56; BB-14 & 104; CT&C-60; QS-176 & 206
One of the best introductory activities; check out the number of book references above. Many variations.

Mrs. O'Grady—I/O, NS, NP
BBA-153; SB-180
A lightweight filler. Not bad for the right group at the right time. Like *Button Pusher,* but not as active.

Name Tag—I/O, MS, NP
QS-207
A name reminder game, where the name of the game absolutely fits.

No. 10 Tin-Can Foot Pass—O, MS, MP
BBA-117
A #10 tin can holds a lot of carrots or corn, so it will easily fit over your shoed foot. How fast can you pass the can around the circle, feet only?

Nuclear Fence—I/O, MS, MP
BB-100; QS-208
This activity takes the place of the black-balled initiative problem called *The Electric Fence*. It's just as challenging and considerably safer.

Nutsy—O, NS, MP
BB-90
You gotta be a bit nutsy to enjoy this one. This is a one time zany activity. Don't play *Nutsy* when you are trying to sell the program.

Object Retrieval—I/O, MS, P
BBA-110
This initiative has become stock-in-trade for many facilitators.

Onion Jousting—I/O, MS, P
BBA-90; QS-178
Got a few extra minutes? Try this one-on-one joust. Good for camps.

Orange Teeth—I/O, NS, MP
BBA-41; SB-147
I have gotten a lot of mileage out of this ascorbic display of ersatz teeth. Matt Rohnke showed me this one when he was in the 4th grade.

Pairs Squared—I/O, S, NP
QS-90
Double your fun with *Pairs Tag*. See below.

Pairs Tag—I/O, S, NP
BBA-2
This is one of those games that doesn't read well but plays great. Also works well with large (100+) groups.

Paper Chute—I/O, NS, MP
QS-179
You need a high (10'+) launching area for this initiative. Good fun sharing defeats, and lends itself to much laughter.

Passing Xed . . .—I/O, NS, MP
BBA-47; SB-55
A classic around-the-campfire "Where's the key?" game.

Paul's Balls Box—I/0, MS, P
SB-21; BBA-109
Can be set up wherever there is an overhead support. People who like basketball find this task irresistible.

PDQ Test—I, NS, NP
SB-172; BBA-151
This is the best series of sit-down activities I know of. Also a very effective way to demonstrate cooperation, communication, trust and fun to administrators and parents.

Peek-A-Who—I/0, NS, P
BBA-10
A unique and hilarious name reminder game. Try the variations.

Phones & Faxes—I/0, MS, P
SB-63
Used to be called *Quail Shooter's Delight*. Same game with a politically correct title. Useful corporate activity.

Pick & Choose—I/0, S, P
SB-77; BBA-51
One of the best decision making games and it moves.

Pick Up Teams—Concept
BBA-170; BB-119
Still choosing up sides by asking the two best athletes or friends to do the honors? There's a better way. See *Categories*.

Ping Pong Pyramids—I, NS, P
QS-181
Useful as an initiative by itself or as part of *The Mastermind Relay*.

Polar Bears . . .—I, NS, MP
BBA-101
Also known as *Pedals Around the Rose*. A vertical/lateral thinking ploy.

Popsicle Push Up—I/0, MS, NP
SB-166; BBA-96
The name militates against itself because the push up position just isn't the way to go. One of my favorite no prop problems.

Porcupine Progression—I/O, NS, MP
BBA-102

If you come up with the answer to this hands on initiative problem, you win. A difficult poser with a satisfying solution.

Quick Line Up—I/O, S, NP/MP
QS-182

The variation requires 4 hula hoops. Effective activity for getting a group to respond efficiently to directions. Few rules, lots of action.

Ready Aim . . .— I/O, S, MP
QS-131

This is great fun. Isn't that enough? Look it up!

Red Baron Stretch—I/O, MS, NP
CT&C-37

Useful for getting ready to participate in an activity where a pre-stretch is necessary. Not your same old bend-at-the-waist stuff.

Retro-Eknhor—I/O, NS, NP
BBA-9

Eknhor is Rohnke spelled backward. How do you pronounce Eknhor? Doesn't matter. A useful introductory activity that causes smiles and confused looks.

Return to the Earth—0, NS, NP
CT&C-41

One of the original Project Adventure warm up activities. Want to see what it used to be like, then return to the earth.

Reversing Pyramid—I/O, NS, NP
BBA-95

Originally a paper and pencil problem. Substitute people for symbols.

Ricochet—I/O, MS, MP
QS-133

A new game that requires a specialized ball. Play in groups of from 2-5. Use the established rules, then make up some of your own. This game lends itself to spontaneous creativity.

Rodeo Throw—I/O, S, P
BBA-33

This is not so much a game as it is a spontaneous happening. Suggest it, don't require it. Don't play on the street.

Rolling Raft Adventure—I, S, P
BBA-107
A specialized initiative problem that requires beau coup tennis balls and other props. Good results if you have the time and gear.

Rope Push—I/O, S, P
BBA-40
This activity is kind of stupid, but that never stopped me before. Change your thinking and sense of accomplishment with this puzzling (contest?).

Samurai Challenge—I/O, S, MP
SB-45; BBA-75
Role playing and histrionic involvement with panache.

Sardines—I, NS, NP
SB-30
This is an OLD game but a favorite of many. Rather than hide and seek, it's seek and hide together; makes for a great ending.

Scooter Slalom—I, S, P
SB-66; BBA-37
Team exhaustion; this is a very active exercise. You need a full gym to set up an "olympic" slalom course, and of course a few gym scooters.

Shark—O, S, P
SB-47; BBA-59
You will need some pre-made props to protect you from the sharks.

Sherpa Walk—O, MS, MP
BBA-16, SB-87
This fantasy walk is a dandy group trust exercise. Set aside at least 30 minutes for the walk, and more for the debrief.

Shoot Out—O, MS, P
SB-39; BBA-61
Fun in the sun (gotta have sun) finding out more about the speed of light and slowness of your hand.

Single Line Potpourri—I/O, S, P
BBA-186
If your ropes course budget is limited, check out the four initiative problems associated with a single swing rope.

Snow Flake—I, NS, MP
SB-145; BBA-39
This should make you laugh even if you just read about it. Playing *Snowflake* from 20+ feet is pure fun. If you don't like *Snowflake* you won't like me.

Sore Spot Tag—I/0, S, NP
BBA-2; See—Hospital Tag
A tag game like *Everybody's It*, but this tag game lasts longer.

Speed Rabbit—I/0, MS, NP
BBA-91; CT&C-63
An introduction to child-like play. I use this animalistic game a lot.

Speedy Gonzalez—0, S, P
MAN
Play some *Italian Golf* then finish up with a running game of *Speedy Gonzalez.*

Spider Web—I/0, MS, P
SB-114 ; QS-209
EVERYBODY knows about the Spider Web initiative. If you don't, better look it up.

Squat Thrust—I/0, MS, NP
SB-94
Introduce this blatantly competitive activity after the group has spent some time developing a sense of trust and cooperation. *Squat Thrust* is definitely more mental than physical.

Squirm—I/0, MS, MP
BBA-33
A one-on-one cooperative exercise utilizing an underinflated beach ball. Emphasizes working together and communicating effectively.

Striker—I/0, S, MP
BBA-88; QS-135
When the key above indicates sweat, it's unequivocal. A full court/full field all out running game.

Subway Sardines—I/0, MS, NP
FS1, See Trust Circle
A trust exercise that should not be attempted until you are sure the group can handle the responsibility for each other's safety.

Stepping Stones—I/O, MS, P
BBA-105; QS—186, See Junk Yard Traverse
Another initiative problem that involves getting from point A
to point B without touching the "poisoned peanut butter."

Swat Tag—I/O, S, P
BB-95
This very active game shows how changing the rules of a
good game can make it even better.

Tangle (Knots, Hands)— I/O, MS, NP/MP
SB-117; See Buddy Ropes
Using hands or *Buddy Ropes* this is a fine portable initiative
that encourages leadership, listening skills, unselfconscious
touch and sense of team.

Tangrams—I, NS, P
SB-129
Rainy day special. Some people have a bent for these creative
puzzle structures; I don't.

Tattoo—I, S, P
SB-22
Almost pure action. Don't look for rationale, it's action/satis-
faction. You need LOTS of tennis balls.

Team Tag Tag—I/O, S, NP
BBA-4
Another warm up tag game with a team affiliation.

Texas Big Foot—I/O, MS, NP
SB-46; BBA-25
Gimmickry, but with the right group and decent timing it's
worth a good laugh and offers effective closure to a game
session.

The Clock—I/O, S, NP
SB-116
A moving initiative based on a Grim(m) nursery rhyme.
Emphasizes individual skills and how to use them effectively.

The Wave—I, S, P
BBA-88
I LOVE this game. That should be enough to entice you to
pick up a copy of BBA and take a look. Use substantial

chairs. The folding gym chairs are at risk during a hot session of *The Wave*.

38 Special—I, NS, P
Bottomless Bag-126
Don't mention the name of this activity during your presentation, 'cause 38's the answer. Answer to what? It's in the book.

Toss-A-Name-Game—I/O, NS, MP
SB-17; BBA-8
This name game should be a prerequisite for all training sessions lasting more than an hour. This is THE game for learning names in the shortest time span.

Touch My Can—I/O, NS, MP
BBA-115
How to be close and not touch. A quickie initiative with a twist.

TP Shuffle & TP Sprint—O, S, P
QS-212
Both of these dynamic initiatives can be attempted separately, but if you plan to use them in tandem, offer the TP Shuffle first.

Traffic Jam—I, NS, MP
SB-122; QS-211
This is not a ten minute initiative. Plan enough time for the problem AND the debrief. Offered in tandem this is an effective and dramatic example of bottom line business at its worst.

Trolley—O, S, P
SB-118; BBA-221; QS-214
There are numerous variations of this classic group initiative. It's worth looking up.

Trust Circle—I/O, MS, NP
QS-233
DO NOT introduce this trust exercise until you feel your group is ready for the responsible self control necessary to insure safety.

Trust Fall/Dive—I/O, NS, P
BBA-19; SB-80; CT&C-53
If you don't know what this is, you haven't been in the field long. Trust falling is a dramatic way to emphasize the need

for trust and to teach spotting in a hands-on manner. Don't discount the *Trust Dive*, it's a natural progression from the *Trust Fall*.

Trust Wave—I/O, MS, NP

QS-234

The *Trust Wave* provides a very visual and physical trust exercise. Keep on top of this one, it's easy for the spotters to become lax.

Turnstile—I/O, S, MP

BBA-116, SB-156; See Hop Box

One of the best "moving" initiatives. *Turnstile* offers an introduction to *Hop Box (Jumping Jack Flash)*.

Tusker—O, S, MP

SB-42

This is a group running game and a variation of *Blob Tag*.

Twirlies—I/O, MS, MP

QS-256

People (all ages) really like *Twirlies*. Use them to kick off an activity period.

Twizzle—I/O, S, NP

QS-137

Requires some memorization on your part, but it's worth it.

2X4—I/O, NS, NP

SB-123

Pull this no-prop initiative out of your pocket when the timing seems right. Collect this type of no-prop initiative for your conceptual bag of tricks.

Two-In-A-Row—I/O, S, P

BBA-116

This is a quick follow up to *Turnstile*.

Unholy Alliance—O, S, P

SB-36; BBA-57

Also called *Four Way Tug-O-War*. This game requires the right venue and some specialized props. Played well, it's an exhausting and revealing exercise.

Up Chuck—O, MS, P

BB-2; BBA-80; QS-191

A variation of *All Catch* with a catchy disgusting name. Can be played equally well with *Twirlies*.

Up Nelson—I, NS, MP
QS-257
After hours game for die hard competitors. It's fun too. You need a long table.

Waiter Wars—O, S, P
QS-139
This is a hot summer day game only—because you're going to get wet.

Warp Speed—I/O, MS, MP
CT&C-83; BBA-53
Warp Speed represents an illusive goal that keeps getting faster and faster as the group makes quantum leap decisions. An initiative problem that draws more from the group than they thought was there.

Waumpum—I/O, MS, MP
BBA-10
A name reminder game with a consequence. It's learn quickly or else.

Whale Watch—O, MS, P
QS-192
Every so often a new ropes course element comes along that captures everyone's imagination. This low element is not only useful but fun too; nice combination.

Where in the Circle Am I?—I/O, NS, NP
QS-92
Here's a decent "getting started" game that encourages group cooperation and the use of names.

Whizzzz Bang—I/O, MS, NP
QS-141
Get psyched, because your presentation style makes or breaks this game. Be the actor.

Whooo . . . ?—O, NS, MP
SB-73 ; BBA-82
Night game. Useful for getting younger people comfortable with the dark in a camp out situation.

"Whoops, Johnny . . . "—I/O, NS, NP
FS1
A "Where's the key" game.

Wordles—I, NS, MP
SB-102, BBA-120
Word play and brainstorming combined. Rainy day and Wordle day; same thing.

Yell—I/O, NS, NP
CT&C-45
"I've yelled in some of the best hotels in the east." An activity that requires some chutzpah on your part, but guaranteed to get an audience's attention.

You Tear Me Up—I, NS, MP
QS-238
A show-and-tell exercise clearly demonstrating that what a group hears isn't necessarily interpreted in the same way. You'll need some scrap paper, all the same size

Your Add—I/O, NS, NP
BBA-48
If you teach arithmetic, this game is golden. If you don't, you'll still like the fast paced action.

Transformer Tag
See Heads & Tails Tag

Tubecide—O, S, P
SB-70
A cold weather game from the early 70's that I haven't played in years, but wish I had. Count on heated action and shedding coats.

Yeah, but . . .—I/O, MS, NP
SB-91; See I Trust You, But . . .

Yurt Rope—I/O, MS, P
QS-258
Based on an activity called *The Yurt Circle*. The rope makes the exercise. Make sure your rope is long and strong enough.

Zits—I/O, S, P
FS1
A swing rope initiative that uses the same numbered gym spots utilized in the initiative problem *Key Punch*.

Zombie—I/O, MS, NP
QS-44
A very loud game that you get to demonstrate. It's a screamer.

Activities by Area

Ice Breakers (IB)
Body Sac
Categories
Caught Ya Peekin'
Chronological Line Up
Comet Balls
Commons
FFEACH
Hog Call
How We Differ
Moon Ball

Warm Up/Deinhibitizer (WU/DI)
Add on Tag
Auto Tag
Bean Bag Tag
Bends, The
Bottoms Up
Bumpity Bump Bump
Patty Cake (Clap Trap)
Cooperative Competition
Coming & Going of the Rain
Dog Shake
Elbow Tag
Everybody's IT
Flip Me the Bird Tag
Have You Ever . . . ?
Heads & Tails Tag
Hog Call
Hopping
Hospital Tag
How're Ya Doin'?
Hustle Handle

Inch Worm
Invisible Jump Rope
It Ain't Me Babe
Knee Slap
Mrs. O'Grady
PDQ
Red Baron Stretch
Retro-Eknhor
Return to the Earth
Sore Spot Tag
Speed Rabbitt
Squat Thrust
Squirm
Toss-A-Name Game
Waumpum
Where In the Circle Am I?
Windmill Stretch

Trust (T)
Balance Broom
Blindfold Cannonball
Blindfold Line Up
Blindfold Soccer
Blind Polygon
Booop
Buddy Ropes
Bump
Coming & Going of the Rain
Commons
Compass Walk
Commandant
Fire in the Hole
Human Camera
Human Ladder
I Trust You, but . . .

Mine Field
Sardines
Scooter Slalom
Sherpa Walk
Speedy Gonzalez
Subway Sardines
The Wave
Toss-A-Name Game
Trust Circle
Trust Fall & Dive
Trust Wave
Whooo . . . ?
Willow in the Whirlwind
Yeah, but . . .
Yell
Yurt Rope
Zombie

Stunts (S)
Cranial Snatch It
Danish Elephants
Dollar Drop
Dollar Jump
Hammeroids
Hansel & Gretel
Look Up/Look Down
Nutsy
Onion Jousting
Orange Teeth
Rodeo Throw
Rope Push
Scooter Slalom
Snow Flake
Squat Thrust
Tattoo
Texas Big Foot
Tubees
Wordles
Yell

Pure Fun Games (PFG)
Ah So Ko
Alienation
Ankle Biters
Asteroids
Back Stabbers
Blindfold Cannonball
Blindfold Soccer
Boffer Bonkers
Bump
Catch 10
Caught Ya Peekin'
Comet Ball Boccie
Comet Balls
Commandant
F Words
Five-A-Side Flatball
Fast Draw
Fire in the Hole
Frog Wars
Funnelator
Help Me Rhonda
Hooper
Italian Golf
Killer
Look Up/Look Down
Monarch
Pairs Squared
Pairs Tag
Phones & Faxes
Ready, Aim . . .
Ricochet
Rolling Raft Adventure
Samurai Challenge
Sardines
Shoot Out
Speed Rabbit
Speedy Gonzalez

Striker
Swar Tag
Team Tag Tag
The Wave
Tusker
Twirles
Twizzle
Unholy Alliance
Up Nelson
Waiter Wars
Whizzz, Bang
Your Add
Zombie

Team Building (TB)

Acronyms
Booop
Bottom Line
Bridge It
Circle The Circle
Claydoughnary
Count Off; 1-20
Dangle Duo Double Use
Don't Touch Me
Frantic
Human Ladder
It Ain't Me Babe
Jumpin' Jack Flash
Kangaroo Catch
Key Punch
Medley Relay
Name Tag
Nesting Balls
Nuclear Fence
Paul's Balls Box
Pick & Choose
Quick Line Up
Rolling Raft Adventure

Sherpa Walk
Tangrams
Traffic Jam
Turnstile
Two in a Row
Warp Speed
Yurt Rope

Initiative Problems (IP)

All Catch
Almost Infinite Circle
Amazon
Balloon Frantic
Balloon Trolleys
Balls Galore
Bang, You're Dead
Blindfold Line Up
Blind Polygon
Bridge It
Bugs in My Cup . . .
Circle the Circle
Count off; 1-20
Dangle Duo Double Use
Diminishing Load
Disc Jockeys
Do-I-Go
Don't Touch Me
Everybody Up
Frantic
Great American Egg Drop
Gooney Likes . . .
Gooney Variations
Group Juggling
Hammeroids
Hands Down
Happy Landings
Human Overhand
Hustle Handle

Impulse Genre
Is This IT?
I've Got the Beat
Jumpin' Jack Flash
Junk Yard
Key Punch
King Me/Queen Me
Maze
Monster
Moon Ball
#10 Ten Can Foot Pass
Nuclear Fence
Object Retrieval
Passing Xed . . .
Paul's Balls Box
Phones & Faxes
Pick & Choose
Ping Pong Pyramids
Polar Bears . . .
Popsicle Push Up
Porcupine Progression
Racoon Rings
Reversing Pyramids
Shark
Single Line Potpourri
Spider Web
Stepping Stones
Tangle (Hands, Knots)
Tangrams
The Clock
Thirty-Eight Special
Touch My Can
TP Shuffle & Sprint
Trolley
Twirlies
Two by Four
Two in a Row

Up Chuck
Warp Speed
Whale Watch
Whoops Johnny
You Tear Me Up
Zits